DID YOU KNOW?

ROBOTS CAN'T DANCE!

and other fun facts

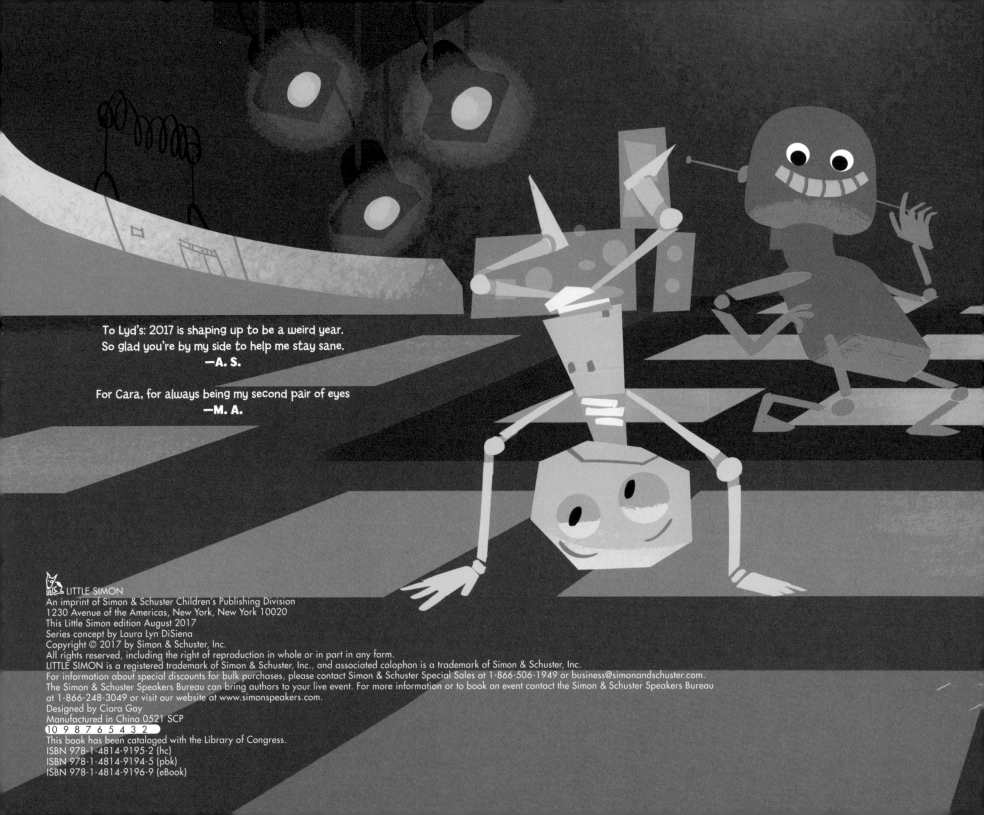

To Lyd's: 2017 is shaping up to be a weird year.
So glad you're by my side to help me stay sane.
—A. S.

For Cara, for always being my second pair of eyes
—M. A.

LITTLE SIMON
An imprint of Simon & Schuster Children's Publishing Division
1230 Avenue of the Americas, New York, New York 10020
This Little Simon edition August 2017
Series concept by Laura Lyn DiSiena
Copyright © 2017 by Simon & Schuster, Inc.
All rights reserved, including the right of reproduction in whole or in part in any form.
LITTLE SIMON is a registered trademark of Simon & Schuster, Inc., and associated colophon is a trademark of Simon & Schuster, Inc.
For information about special discounts for bulk purchases, please contact Simon & Schuster Special Sales at 1-866-506-1949 or business@simonandschuster.com.
The Simon & Schuster Speakers Bureau can bring authors to your live event. For more information or to book an event contact the Simon & Schuster Speakers Bureau
at 1-866-248-3049 or visit our website at www.simonspeakers.com.
Designed by Ciara Gay
Manufactured in China 0521 SCP
10 9 8 7 6 5 4 3 2
This book has been cataloged with the Library of Congress.
ISBN 978-1-4814-9195-2 (hc)
ISBN 978-1-4814-9194-5 (pbk)
ISBN 978-1-4814-9196-9 (eBook)

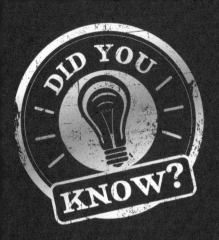

DID YOU KNOW?

ROBOTS CAN'T DANCE!

and other fun facts

By Hannah Eliot

Illustrated by Aaron Spurgeon
and Mauricio Abril

LITTLE SIMON

New York   London   Toronto   Sydney   New Delhi

TYPEWRITER! PEPPERROOT! PIROUETTER!

Oh—hey! Those aren't just random words up there. Did you know that each of those is a 10-letter word that can be typed using only the top row of a standard English keyboard? And although we normally think of computers as machines that sit on desks or in our laps, small computers are also embedded into other objects such as cell phones, microwaves, toys, and even . . . ROBOTS. Did you know that?

Wait, you did? Well, did you know that ROBOTS CAN'T DANCE?! Here's the thing: There are some really cool robots out there. For example, one robot called PaPeRo can talk and control household devices. It can memorize up to 30 different faces and tell them apart!

NO MORE QUESTIONS, PLEASE!

Then there's AIBO, a robot that looks like a dog! It has sensors on its head, back, chin, and paws. Each AIBO starts as a newborn puppy and then develops its own personality based on how it is raised—just like a real dog.

And then there's a robot called QRIO that has foot sensors so it can play soccer. It can even pick itself up after falling and check itself for damage! Qrio can also dance!

Well, that's confusing. Isn't the title of this book *Robots Can't Dance!*? Actually, a lot of robots *can*. But those robots are *programmed* to dance. You see, we use the word "robot" to mean any MAN-MADE machine that can do work or perform other actions normally done by humans. So up to this point in time, robots don't have the amazing ability that *we* have of being able to create and perfect dances on our own. But who knows what the future holds!

Robots can, however, do tons of other cool things. Today most robots are used for repetitive actions or jobs that are considered too dangerous for humans. Robots can perform complicated surgical operations, they can play you in chess, and they can even go into OUTER SPACE!
They can do this because they have what's called "artificial intelligence"—or "AI" for short. It's true. Some computers and robots have been programmed with the ability to *act* like humans!

Did you know that the average person blinks 20 times a minute, but when they're in front of a computer, their blinking slows to only 7 times a minute? How about that the computer MOUSE is called that because its inventors thought the wire coming out of it looked like mouse's tail?!

And we can't talk about a computer without talking about the INTERNET. In the 1960s, a scientist proposed a system through which computers could "talk" to one another. Scientists and researchers started sending data and files to one another, but things really changed in 1989 when the World Wide Web was created. The Internet was no longer just a place to send and receive files; it was now a "web" of information that anyone using the Internet could access. Today, the Internet is used for research, business, online shopping, news, social networking, and so much more. Also thanks to the Internet, a whole new language of Internet slang was born.
LOL! JK! BRB! TTYL!

TTYL? No, we're talking now! Have you heard of Alexander Graham Bell? He is credited as the INVENTOR of the telephone, although not everyone agrees that's true. He did, however, get the first patent for a telephone in 1876. More than 100 years later—in 1983—the first mobile phones went on sale in the United States. In those hundred years, the phone went through lots of different changes!

There was the candlestick phone,

the rotary phone,

the touch-tone phone,

the portable phone,

and finally, the mobile phone.

And did you know that the first mobile phone weighed nearly 2 pounds? That's like carrying a pineapple around with you!

Did you know that in Japan, about 90 percent of cell phones sold are WATERPROOF . . . so they can be used in the shower? It's a good thing, because guess what? A cell phone carries 10 times more bacteria than a toilet seat! YUCK!

Some of us listen to music on our phones. And some of us listen to the radio! Did you know that radio waves are *not* sound waves? They carry sounds, but they're actually electromagnetic waves that travel FASTER than the speed of sound!

These days, there are lots of forms of entertainment: movies, computer games, video games, and more. But did you know that between the 1920s and 1950s radio was one of the most popular forms of entertainment? There were radios in most homes! Kids and parents would gather around to listen to their favorite shows: comedies, dramas, game shows, popular music shows, and more.

There were—and are—ways to listen to music other than on a phone or on the radio. Have you heard of the PHONOGRAPH? Well, it was invented by Thomas Edison, who also invented the lightbulb! The phonograph was known as a "talking machine." That's because it could record *and* replay sound. This gave way to the development of records! Then came cassette tapes, portable stereos, CDs, and MP3 players. Did you know that the typical length of the tape inside a cassette tape is about 280 feet? That would reach as high as 50 cows stacked on top of one another!

We hear sound from a television, too. But unlike music players, the television also receives and displays IMAGES! Did you know that what you're watching on TV is actually just a series of individual pictures? Did you know that for the first 30 years after the television was invented, TVs could only show black-and-white images?

Did you know that soccer's FIFA World Cup is the world's most widely viewed sporting event, since billions of viewers are able to watch it on TV?

Television shows are one thing you watch on-screen. Can you name something else? Think: popcorn, candy, and cushy seats. That's right, movies! Now, you've probably seen an animated movie, but do you really know what animation is? It's the art of making *inanimate* objects appear to move. An inanimate object is something that is not living. Look around—do you see any inanimate objects? How about a chair? A sandwich? A sneaker? Something else you might not know about animation is that the movement is actually created by putting together a sequence of still pictures that are each slightly different.

Have you ever seen a 3-D movie? A 3-D film actually TRICKS your brain into thinking that flat images are three-dimensional. Pick an object near you right now. Close only your left eye. Your right eye can see more to the right than it can to the left. Now close your right eye. Your left eye can see more to the left than it can to the right. Now open both eyes. Your brain combines these images from both eyes, allowing you to see in THREE DIMENSIONS! This is also known as stereoscopic vision. Films in 3-D use this technique so that you can *see* in 3-D on an otherwise flat screen. How cool is that?!

Have you flown on a plane before? Did you watch any movies while flying? Today, planes have way more advanced technology than in 1878, when flight was just the dream of two kids. That's when 7-year-old Orville Wright and his 11-year-old brother, Wilbur, began to build and test an airplane. On December 17, 1903, the Wright brothers became the first people to fly a machine that was heavier than a hot-air balloon and under the complete controls of a pilot. The flight only lasted 12 seconds, but it worked!

Did you know that the only living things capable of TRUE FLIGHT are insects, birds, and bats? And while flying fish don't technically fly, they *can* glide for hundreds of feet due to their extra-large fins that act like wings.

There's also the flying snake. These snakes can be as long as 4 feet! But it's one of the smallest ones, the paradise tree snake, that's the best glider. This snake has been known to travel up to 330 feet through the air! That's as high as the Statue of Liberty in New York and Big Ben in London, though not quite as high as the Great Pyramid of Giza in Egypt!

We all know that cars don't fly, but right now FLYING CARS are being developed! How long do you think it will be before we all fly in cars? Your guess is as good as any! Did you know that one of the first cars sold to the public, Karl Benz's Motorwagen, could only go up to 10 miles per hour? You could run faster than that car could go! Did you know that the Volkswagen Beetle got its name because it looks like a bug? Did you know that the first official car race was in 1895 in France? And that modern race cars can go up to about 220 miles per hour?

Can you think of some ways cars HELP us today? How about ambulances that respond to emergencies, trucks that bring food to the grocery store (or toys to the toy store, or packages to our homes), police cars that help make sure we're safe, taxis that get us where we need to go, buses that take us on tours around new cities, and more!

Cars these days use tons of different technologies. Most have seat warmers, air-conditioning, windows that electronically go up and down, air bags, and more. And how about GPS? Throughout history, our ancestors had different ways to make sure they didn't get lost. They built huge monuments and landmarks that they'd be able to see from a distance, they created extremely detailed maps, and they learned to read stars in the night sky. Today, it's practically *impossible* to get lost, thanks to GPS!

GPS stands for Global Positioning System. It works by using about 30 SATELLITES that are up in space, orbiting the Earth. These satellites send radio waves down to Earth, and our GPS devices pick up these waves. A GPS device requires waves from 4 different satellites to determine its position.

So satellites send radio waves to our GPS devices, and as you learned before, a radio wave is a type of electromagnetic wave. Want to know something else that uses electromagnetic waves? X-RAYS! If you think of doctors when you think of X-rays, you're on the right track! X-rays were developed to be used in medicine. But do you know how they work? Here's how: The X-ray waves can easily pass through air and body tissue. But when those waves encounter a material that's denser, like bone or even metal fragments, those waves are stopped. The rays that *can* pass through the body hit a photographic plate. Once the photograph has been processed, the air shows up as BLACK, the soft tissue shows up as GRAY, and the denser material shows up as WHITE—since the rays couldn't get through it. Pretty cool, right?

But X-rays aren't just used in doctors' offices! Telescopes that detect X-rays have been sent into space, allowing us to make discoveries beyond our own solar system. X-rays have also allowed scientists and art historians to see "underpaintings"—literally, what's *under* a painting! Because they're able to see sketches the artist used as guides, X-rays have helped these art historians understand the way artists worked. X-rays have also allowed us to study valuable artifacts such as Egyptian MUMMIES to see what's inside!

And just as many artists sketch on a canvas before painting on top of it, the camera is another tool that has been helping artists for a long time. But maybe not in the way that you think. You see, before the cameras we have today, there was something called the "camera obscura." This was basically a dark box—or even a dark room—with a hole in it. When an object or scene was placed *outside* the hole, the light would pass through it, strike a surface inside, and then project an image onto another surface. That second surface might have been a piece of paper or a canvas. An artist could then trace the projected image and draw or paint on top of that.

So how does a modern camera work? Well, when you press the button to take a photo, it briefly opens the "shutter." Think of it like opening a curtain. This allows light to pass through the camera lens and onto the film, or sensor, inside. During the day or when it's BRIGHT out, the shutter may only open for 1/200th of a second! At night, or when it's DARK out, the shutter stays open longer to allow more light into the camera.

Pretty much all the technology we've covered so far requires ENERGY.
Energy is the ability to do work. That work might be moving, warming, lighting, or powering something.
Renewable energy is sometimes called "green energy" because it comes from natural sources
that are continuously replenished. Renewable energy is great for many reasons. Since it's renewable,
we won't run out of it. And because it's natural, it doesn't pollute or hurt our land, air, or water.

There are different types of renewable energy. SOLAR ENERGY comes from the sun. Energy that comes from moving water is called HYDROPOWER. And there's also GEOTHERMAL energy, which comes from the heat inside the Earth. Miles below Earth's surface lies melted rock called "magma." In certain areas just below Earth's crust, there are pools of water that get super hot from the heat that rises from the magma. And *sometimes* the hot water even bursts through cracks in the crust and forms what we call geysers, shooting water and steam into the air! Old Faithful in Yellowstone National Park is one of the most famous geysers.

Energy and electricity play a big role in the construction of new buildings. In fact, pretty much all of the technology we've talked about so far plays a role in construction. Computers help architects create the plans for a building. Cars and trucks transport materials to the site. Workers may communicate by phone or radio. Cameras are used to take photographs of the building's progress. And construction technology is constantly developing. For example, there's 3-D printing for concrete, solar roads that could actually *create* energy, and drones that help us survey the land.

Look around your neighborhood, or your town, or your city, and you'll probably notice at least *some* sort of construction project. Homes, office buildings, schools, and more are being built. Advancements in the technology of phones, computers, and even robots are being made every day. And that's because the world around you is constantly changing and growing—just like you!
But unlike robots, bet you sure can DANCE!

MORE FUN FACTS

Robot: A robot called Paro was modeled after a baby harp seal, and it responds to cuddling!

Computer: The first computer bug ever was *actually* a bug! In 1947, computer scientist Grace Hopper found a moth in her computer that was causing an error!

Airplane: In 1932, Amelia Earhart became the first woman to fly solo across the Atlantic Ocean!

Internet: The term "surfing the Internet" was coined by a librarian!

X-ray: Wilhelm Röntgen was the first person to observe X-rays, and he won the first Nobel Prize in physics in 1901!

Construction: Currently the tallest building in the world is the Burj Khalifa in Dubai. It is 2,716 feet tall. It took 6 *years* to build. In 2011, Alain "Spiderman" Robert took 6 hours to scale the outside of it!

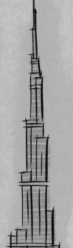

Music: Music may be good for your heart! Studies suggest that listening to music can trigger real changes that affect your blood pressure, heart rate, and breathing.

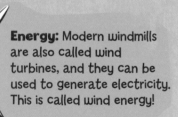

Animation: Mickey Mouse was originally called Mortimer Mouse, but Walt Disney's wife convinced him to change it to Mickey!

Phone: The first cell phone cost $4,000!

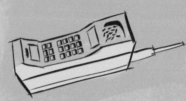

Energy: Modern windmills are also called wind turbines, and they can be used to generate electricity. This is called wind energy!

Television: The first remote control was released in the 1950s and it was called Lazy Bones.

GPS: There are now GPS shoes! GPS SmartSole is an insert you can put in your shoe, so if you get lost, someone can track you!

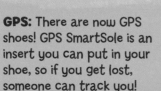

Car: 35% of the world's population drives on the left side of the road.

Camera: "Photography" comes from the Greek words "photos," which means light, and "graphos," which means to draw.